T0146806

ON THE GOLF COURSE

101

WAYS TO ROCK YOUR WORLD

IMPROVE YOUR GAME ONE TIP AT A TIME

Other books by Dayna Steele

*101 Ways to Rock Your World: Everyday
Activities for Success Every Day*

*Rock to the Top: What I Learned about Success
from the World's Greatest Rock Stars*

ON THE GOLF COURSE

101

WAYS TO ROCK YOUR WORLD

IMPROVE YOUR GAME ONE TIP AT A TIME

"Not only a must-read for every golfer and wannabe golfer, but should be required equipment in every golf bag for quick reference and laughter."

—Joe Pogge, host, *Smokin' Joe's Driving Range*, CBS Sports Radio

DAYNA STEELE
With PGA Pro Aram Hudson and Cathy Arroyo
Illustrated by Tim Griggs

iUniverse LLC
Bloomington

ON THE GOLF COURSE
101 Ways to Rock Your World

iUniverse books may be ordered through booksellers or by contacting:

iUniverse
1663 Liberty Drive
Bloomington, IN 47403
www.iuniverse.com
1-800-Authors (1-800-288-4677)

Because of the dynamic nature of the Internet, any web addresses or
links contained in this book may have changed since publication and
may no longer be valid. The views expressed in this work are solely those
of the author and do not necessarily reflect the views of the publisher,
and the publisher hereby disclaims any responsibility for them.

Any people depicted in stock imagery provided by Thinkstock are models,
and such images are being used for illustrative purposes only.

Certain stock imagery © Thinkstock.

ISBN: 978-1-9389-0846-0 (sc)
ISBN: 978-1-9389-0847-7 (e)

Library of Congress Control Number: 2013916862

Printed in the United States of America.

iUniverse rev. date: 10/18/2013

This book does not guarantee your golf game will get any
better. Only the magic golf fairy can do that and we have
not found her yet. We will continue to look for her.

To Charlie, my favorite golf partner always.
And to the three who round out the foursome
in my life—Cris, Dack, and Nick.

Born to golf. Forced to work.

—Unknown

Contents

Foreword

After taking on the game of golf at the tender age of thirteen, I have enjoyed (or agonized over) this worldly game for fifty-four years. Not without some measure of success, mind you, but unless you are Jack Nicklaus or Tiger Woods, you will enjoy, or suffer, a miniscule amount of winning occasions and far more agonizing defeats. Fleeting are the wins, and devastating are the losses.

Given that this is true, one must develop a strong, immensely fierce sense of humor, complete with predictable one-liners after every sodded tee shot, giant slice, or pull hook. Not to mention a repertoire of curse words in several different languages that fly out of your mouth faster than a gnat can be sucked into your nose on a spring evening. That being said, there is no limit to the creativity of unsavory words exhaled by the p----d-off hack—or professional, for that matter.

Dayna has absolutely captured a great deal of the flavor of this great game in this book. If you have ever played the game with any degree of sincerity, the book will remind you of the exhilarating successes, beauty, and humor that only the game of golf can provide in abundance.

—**Hal Underwood**, professional golfer

About Hal Underwood

Hal Underwood made a statement to the collegiate golfing world as a first-team all-American at the University
of Houston in 1967 and 1968. He consistently placed
in NCAA tournament play and won the All-American
Intercollegiate in 1967 and 1968. Underwood also won
the 1967 Border Olympics, the 1967 Morris Williams
Tournament, and the 1967 Eastern and Trans-Mississippi
events. Underwood left the University of Houston
thirteen hours shy of a degree and turned professional
in 1969. His career as a playing professional was high-
lighted by winning two events on the Australian Tour
(Otago Golf Classic, Queensland Open) in 1977. He also
won the Portland Open in 1975 and lost in a playoff to
Gary Player in the Jacksonville Open of 1971.

Texas golf lore has it that Underwood was the inspi-
ration for Kevin Costner's character in the hit film
Tin Cup. These days you can find him instructing at
the Advantage School of Golf in Kingwood, Texas.
Underwood's pupils have included Billy Ray Brown,
Mark Lye, Steve Elkington, and author Dayna Steele,
who does Underwood's signature "waggle" better than
the others.

Acknowledgments

When I sat down to write *101 Ways to Rock Your World: Everyday Activities for Success Every Day*, it was fun to compile the list of things that followed the FastCompany.com Expert Perspectives blog post "5 Things to Do Every Day for Success." Never in my wildest imagination did I think I had created a book series that would take on a life of its own. There are literally dozens of adaptations in work or rolling around in my head, not to mention a product line of T-shirts and coffee mugs and even a possible daily cartoon strip.

All of this does not manifest in my brain without help. It started with someone (I wish I remembered who said it first) commenting that *101 Ways to Rock Your World: Everyday Activities for Success Every Day* was like "Chicken Soup for the Soul for the Twitter Generation." That was followed by an offhand remark made by one of my iUniverse editors as we worked on that first book, "This could be a never-ending series like 'For Dummies.'" Well, I don't need much more to kick me into entrepreneurial action, and I sincerely thank both of these people for creating this monster.

My thanks to Sid Arroyo for having the good sense to marry Cathy Arroyo, and by doing so, providing me with my first female golf partner and now dear friend. An avid golfer, she agreed to help with this book, guiding me through the initial tips to the final edits. Cathy also "loaned" me her golfer family, Jennifer Guido and Jim Zorn, to go over the early tips and add their golf insight.

Thanks also to Aram Hudson, my PGA teaching pro, who expressed an interest in writing a book and was thus recruited into the process, creating even more tips and organizing the entire thing into the beginnings of a book. Not to mention trying to perfect my swing along the way. I swear the only thing I have heard Aram say for over a year is, "Hips, Dayna, hips, move your hips."

I am often asked if it was hard to write a book. "No," I reply, "that is the easy part." The hard part is the editing, rewriting, editing again, correcting, editing, crying, correcting again, planning, marketing, and production. That is the hard work, and it helps to have an incredible team that jumps right in to help: Susan McCoy Neuhalfen, for press and more editing; Eylat Poliner, for working diligently as a remote admin on lists, keywords, and anything else I throw her way; and as always, Wilene Dunn, my speech and appearance booking partner. I even bought her golf lessons, hoping to pull her into this crazy sport with me so we could play as we travel around the country speaking at conferences.

To the many people I have played golf with and who have tolerated my average game and disruptive antics on the golf course: neither will probably ever improve, and I appreciate the fact you still let me play.

The fun continues, and I thank you, the reader, for enabling my writing, and now golf, addiction.

Golf is a precision club and ball sport, in which competing players (or golfers) use many types of clubs to hit balls into a series of holes on a golf course using the fewest number of strokes.

—Definition from Wikipedia

The Warm-Up

Charlie, also known as Wonder Husband, bought me a beginner's set of golf clubs for Mother's Day in 2005. This was not a gift I had ever expressed any interest in receiving. Never. Zero. Period. Nada. Zilch. I was not a happy mommy.

In the 1970s, I grew up on the Quail Valley Golf Club course in Missouri City, Texas. I tried their junior lessons once and declared it a stupid game. About as close as I came to the golf course the rest of my teenage years was to drive the beer cart for a couple of major tournaments that were held at Quail Valley during that time.

As my rock radio career launched after college, any sort of sport was the furthest thing from my mind. When many of the 1980s' "hair bands" took up golf, I thought they were nuts to play what I had declared a stupid game. It was entertaining, though, to watch staid and stuffy golf course facilities try to figure out what to do with the likes of Alice Cooper, Van Halen, and Def Leppard (all very good golfers).

That first set of Mother's Day clubs was followed that same year by a gift certificate for lessons on my birthday and a golf club travel case at Christmas. That was when I became a reluctant golfer. I decided that if Charlie wanted his wife to play golf that badly, especially when the stereotype dictates that most men seem to play to get away from their wives, then I had better at least pretend to like it. I know, a stereotype, but deal with it since, for the most part, it is true.

Six months into this charade, I discovered I was addicted to the game. I was on my way home from a meeting and stopped at a local golf superstore to buy a new club. I did not need a new club—I still was not really sure what to do with the ones I had—but I just knew if I bought this one club, my game would be better. As I walked to the car with my shiny new purchase, the realization hit me: "I have caught the disease. I am a golfer."

Since that time, I have learned to relax and enjoy the game as well as the process. Once I realized there were no "golf police," I relaxed. That, and I stopped being intimidated once I also realized just about everybody who plays the game lies about their game. You know who you are.

When you gain the courage to admit you play golf, friends and old acquaintances come out of the closet to admit they have the addiction as well. You are never at a loss for someone to play with. Rockers, intellectuals, wallflowers—people you never in a million years would have thought played golf—have a set of clubs just waiting for a golf outing.

It has now become just as much a part of my life as eating, sleeping, and writing. I think more than anything, I enjoy the time with my wonderful husband, Charlie. We talk, we laugh, we curse, we commiserate, and we share during this game we love. We schedule vacations and work trips around golf courses if at all possible. I even built a tee box and putting green in the backyard for Charlie's sixtieth birthday. Okay, maybe it was a little bit of a gift for me too. And as we start to design our golden years, every image of that retirement and every location considered tend to include a golf course.

I have many new shiny clubs now and find myself dreaming that a new set of irons would fix everything. I officially now have more golf clothes than rock clothes in my closet. I still think it is a stupid game, but now it is a stupid game I cannot seem to get enough of. Need someone to fill out your foursome? I'm your gal.

Fore!

They call it golf because all the other four-letter words were taken.

—Raymond Floyd, professional golfer

Psychology

Golf is more exacting than racing, cards, speculation, or matrimony. In almost all other games, you pit yourself against a mortal foe. In golf, it is yourself against the world; no human being stays your progress as you drive your ball over the face of the Earth.

—Arnold Haultain,
The World of Golf

1. Visualize the course before you play.

Picture yourself hitting the ball right where you know it needs to go. See your amazing short game as well as your putts fall into the hole in this visualization. Think of this as golf meditation and envision your success on the course. Sweet dreams!

2. Arrive early.

When you are in a calm and prepared state of mind, you play better. When you are rushed and agitated, you are not going to like your first shot or many others that follow that first one. The calmer you are, the better you play.

3. Set tangible goals.

Maybe it is that one putt you cannot seem to make or that one body of water you cannot seem to get over. Set smaller, obtainable goals; and as you achieve those goals, set the bar a little higher.

I have an insane desire to shave a stroke or two off my handicap.

> —**Alistair Cooke,** golfer and television
> personality, on why he was retiring
> as host of *Masterpiece Theater*

4.   Be in the moment.

Enjoy the beauty of nature and what is around you. Turn off your phone and quit worrying about the rest of the world. Half of the game of golf is taking in your surroundings to plan for your next great shot.

The only time my prayers are never answered is on the golf course.

—Billy Graham,
Christian evangelist
and golfer

5. Create your own confidence.

Tell yourself you can and will have a good game. The first step to being a rock star is believing you are a rock star. Belief plus preparation and visualization will make you a confident golfer. Never use the word *can't*.

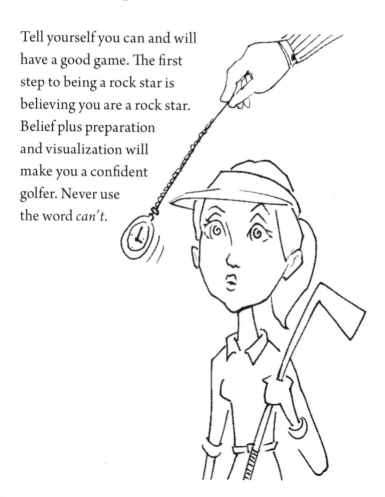

6. Forget the last shot.

Good or bad ... there is nothing you can do about it anymore. Unless, of course, you can time travel—and if you can, we need to talk.

7. Do not count penalties.

For casual games, this will make the game more fun for you and keep your blood pressure in check. It makes the game go faster as well. It is okay to do this; there really are no golf course police watching you keep score.

The simpler I keep things, the better I play.

—**Nancy Lopez,** professional golfer

8. Research the course.

Take a look at the course website and study the layout. Google the course name and see what other golfers have to say about the course. Ask friends and fellow golfers what they know about the course. You can never go wrong with preparation, homework, and information. Ask the starter for course tips. And never forget to ask where the bathroom is!

9. Match the tee box to your ability.

This is a great training tool to help you gain confidence and learn to shoot a birdie, a hole played in one shot under par. As you become consistent with your birdies and your confidence increases, move back a tee. By the way, never call the most forward tees the "ladies' tees."

It took me seventeen years to get 3,000 hits in baseball. I did it in one afternoon on the golf course.

—**Hank Aaron,** one of Major
League Baseball's all-time
greats and golfer

10. Do not blame the club.

The club hits the ball in exactly the manner you swing it and where you aim it. It is usually not the club's fault. Throwing the club in the water or trying to break it in half will definitely not make it any better either. Be nice to your club—unless it is from 1973; then blame the club.

My handicap? Woods and irons.

>   —**Chris Codiroli,** MLB player and golfer

11. Ignore swing thoughts while you play.

Take your practice swing. Then step up to the ball and swing already. The best players see a target and hit the ball there. Concentrate on where you want the ball to go, not so much on how you are going to get it there.

Papa, trust your swing.

—Note written by ten-year-old **Qass Singh** and pinned to professional golfer **Vijay Singh's** golf bag during the 2000 US Masters, which the elder Singh won

12. Keep a golf journal.

Count how many times you have hit the ball on different parts of the course: fairway hits, putts per hole, and GIRs (greens in regulation). This helps identify the next thing you need to work on in your game, or it confirms you are currently working on what needs work. Also write down goals, epiphanies, successes, challenges, and fun stories. Who knows? You might have a golf book some day!

Greens in regulation (GIR): A green is considered hit "in regulation" if any part of the ball is touching the putting surface and the number of strokes taken is at least two fewer than par (i.e., by the first stroke on a par 3, the second stroke on a par 4, or the third stroke on a par 5). Greens-in-regulation percentage is one of many statistics kept by the PGA Tour.

—Wikipedia

13. Emphasize the good.

Create a *Good* and a *Bad* column for every game, and then mark down every shot you take. You may be surprised by the ratio at the end of your round. You reinforce whatever you focus on—so focus on what you did well. You never know when you will find that elusive birdie or eagle. That is what keeps all of us going back to the golf course again and again.

A bad day of golf is better than a good day of meetings.

—**Charlie Justiz,** pilot, author, and golfer

Strategy

Try to think where you want to put the ball, not where you don't want it to go.

—**Billy Casper,** professional golfer

14. Separate practice from play.

Both need to be performed differently because the end results can be so very different. Try playing on one day and practicing on another. The swing you bring to the course is the swing you will have that day.

15. Practice putting before a round.

Practice putting different lengths and directions. Even putts on the same greens have different speeds. This will give you an idea of how the course is running that day— slow, fast, wet, or dry. Plus, if you can putt, you can golf.

You don't necessarily have to be a good golfer to be a good putter, but you do have to be a good putter to be a good golfer.

—**Tony Lema,** professional golfer

16. Play a "one of two best balls" format.

The first ball you hit is "Player A." Your second shot is "Player B." Pay attention to which ball worked best for you. Play the best shot, picking up the other ball and dropping it next to that best ball. Then do it again and again. When other golfers are involved, this is most often referred to as a "scramble." Only do this if time allows and you are not holding up golfers behind you.

I have a tendency to remember my poor shots a shade more vividly than the good ones.

—**Ben Hogan,** professional golfer

17. Think strategically, like a chess player.

Chess players always try to make a move that sets them up for the next anticipated move. Chess players think one move ahead. Do the same with your golf game: figure out where is the best place for your current shot so that you can make the most of your next shot after that. This goes for all of your shots—fairways, greens, and putts. You do not have to play well to score well.

18. Create a preshot routine.

Every tour pro has one; there is no reason you should not have one as well. It can be as simple as the way you walk up to the ball, the way you picture where you want the ball to go, and how you line up the shot. Just make sure it is the same every time.

I play in the low 80s. If it is any hotter than that, I won't play.

—**Joe E. Louis,** comedian, singer, and golfer

19. Practice trouble shots.

The course does not give you perfect, flat lies. If you really want to get some good practice, drop the ball into trouble situations (uphill and downhill lies, sand, etc.) on the range and practice getting out of that trouble. Great players became great by learning how to manipulate their golf ball. Never be afraid to experiment.

The number-one thing about trouble is ... don't get into more.
— **Dave Stockton,** professional golfer

20. Learn from every round.

After every round, good or bad, ask yourself what you have learned that round. Take that knowledge to your next game or practice. Make some notes in that golf journal you now have. Taking something away from every round turns that round into a success regardless of how well you played.

I never learned anything from a match that I won.

—**Robert Trent Jones Jr.,** golf course architect and golfer

21. Increase your driver loft.

Too many amateurs try to play an 8.5 to 9.5 loft because it is what the pros do. Ask your local PGA pro what loft he or she would suggest and make that change. You will notice the difference immediately in the quality of your drive.

Let's get after it.

> —**Rose Montgomery's** signature expression
> after spitting on her gloves at the start of a
> round. On June 2, 1992, she hit her tenth
> career hole-in-one at Canyon Country Club
> in Palm Springs—at the age of ninety-six.

Why are eighteen holes played in golf?

Legend has it there are eighteen shots in a
bottle of scotch whiskey, just enough for a
shot a hole. Many have debunked this myth,
but we refuse to acknowledge their facts!

22. Buy a yardage book.

Most courses offer a yardage book for their particular course. There are also apps for your phone for many of these courses. Do you navigate in a big city without a map or GPS? You will noticeably see your game improve.

23. Learn your clubs.

Keep track of the club you used, the length of your swing, and the yardage you hit in your golf journal. Over time, you will see a pattern and have a better idea of what club to grab for which yardage. Never worry about how far someone else hits with the same club. It is different for everyone, and what really matters is the final score. Knowing how far each club goes is crucial to scoring.

24. Practice the shots you dislike.

Head out to the driving range and use your neglected clubs, practicing the shots you do not like to make with those clubs you never use. You never know when that practice might create another best shot or favorite club.

25. Video record your swing.

Just about everyone has a video capability on his or her mobile phone these days. Ask your golf buddy to record your swing. Take a look when you get back home and compare it to some of the pros' online. It will be like an instant mini-lesson.

26. Play *your* game.

Lessons are good. Helpful advice from your fellow golfers is nice. The best thing to do, however, is to play what you know works for you. You'll learn this from practicing and playing this crazy game. This is how you will score the best. Do not be afraid to fail—in golf or anything; it is how you learn to be better and have the most fun with the least frustration—at anything.

Forget your opponents, always play against par.

—**Sam Snead,** professional golfer

27. Practice short-game shots.

Take small, medium, and large swings to get a feel for your short game with each of your short-game clubs. Get to know your short-game shots and watch the strokes melt away from your game. Your short-game technique should be completely different from your full-swing technique. And that technique is different for each player.

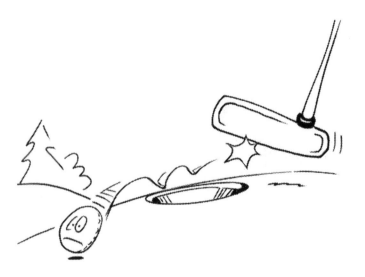

28. Practice bunker shots.

Your club never actually touches the ball on a correctly executed sand shot. If you know how to use the bounce and practice this shot, you will be able to get out of the bunker almost every time! A good saying to remember is "You can't get the ball out if you don't get the sand out."

No golfer can ever become too good to practice.

—**May Hezlet,** British amateur golfer

29. Take your medicine.

Do not try to be the golfer or golf superhero you are not. Admit you are in trouble and take that "medicine" shot to get you back into the game and out of trouble. Remember the mantra, "One into trouble, one out of trouble."

30. Find the short grass.

Play for fairways and greens whenever you can. The short grass is always better than the high grass. Period. Of course, high grass is better than sand, trees, water, and alligators.

31. Know where to miss.

Every course has bailout areas; know where they are on the holes that challenge you. For example, if there is a water hazard, play around the water hazard. You may have to take extra shots, but if all goes well, you will not have to use extra balls. If you learn to curve the ball, curve it away from the trouble.

Hit it hard. It will land somewhere.

—**Mark Calcavecchia,** professional golfer

32. Play smart golf.

Keep the ball in play and out of trouble. Do not try a shot out of the rough through the trees for maximum distance if there is a clear shot to the fairway. Do not aim for the pin over water and sand if there is an unobstructed shot to any other part of the green. Play the course; do not let the course play you—it will win every time!

33. Putt when you can.

You do not have to chip each time you are near the green. As a casual golfer, you will almost always do better with your putter than when you try to chip the ball onto the green.

A man who can putt is a match for anyone.
—**Willie Park,** professional golfer

34. Take lessons.

Learning takes place from proper feedback. Your local PGA Pro is your best source for feedback about your game. Learn a lesson from this: even the pros take lessons. Remember, new lessons pay off better than new clubs.

If you expect a miracle, you should expect to pay for one.

—**Derek Hardy,** golf coach who charges $1,000 for one lesson and $140 for thirteen lessons

Etiquette

Play the ball as it lies, play the course as you find it, and if you cannot do either, do what is fair.

—Back of the official United States Golf Association rules book

35. Know the rules and etiquette of golf.

At the very least, it shows you have a passion for the game, as well as respect for your fellow golfers and the course. You can find the complete list at http://www.usga.org/ etiquette/tips/Golf-Etiquette-101/.

36. Be quiet and considerate of others.

Golf is a great game played with others, but remember to keep that camaraderie to a minimum when someone else is hitting. Any noise, including talking, ringing phones, or loud food wrappers, can distract a golfer as he or she hits the ball. Your best bet? Learn to tune out the noise so that nothing bothers you.

It is good sportsmanship to not pick up lost golf balls while they are still rolling.

—**Mark Twain,** author, humorist, and golfer

37. Leave the course better than you found it.

Take care of every course you play: replace divots, fix pitch marks, pick up trash, only drive carts where designated, let the staff know if there is a problem on the course, etc. Ever heard of karma? Feed the golf gods every chance you get.

It can be asserted with total confidence that one of the most important reasons why we golfers believe golf to be the finest of all games is that it is played in beautiful surroundings.

—**Peter Dobereiner,** *Golf Digest* writer
and golfer

38. Be aware of the putting line.

Be conscious of where the other golfer's putting line lies. Do not walk across that line or let your shadow fall over the line while he or she is putting. Also, do not scuff your golf shoes on the green, disturbing the grass. The green is always sacred ground.

The mind messes up more shots than the body.

—**Tommy Bolt,** professional golfer

39. Keep up the pace.

Keep up with the golfers in front of you without crowding them. Your play should average about fifteen minutes per hole. Ask the starter if this is consistent with the course expectations.

On 18, you've got to drive it up a gnat's ass.

—**Greg Norman,** professional golfer

40. Let faster players play through.

If you are holding up play, and time allows on the course, offer to let smaller or faster groups behind you play through.

41. Watch your swing path and theirs.

A trip to the emergency room can really put a damper on any golf game. Make sure you are aware of your fellow golfers and their swing paths as well as your own.

You swing your best when you have the fewest things to think about.

—**Bobby Jones,** professional golfer

42. Praise other golfers.

Everyone likes to be praised. Jealous or snarky comments are just plain ugly on anyone. Being humble gains you respect and makes you a better golf buddy.

Golf is a compromise between what your ego wants you to do, what experience tells you to do, and what your nerves let you do.

—**Bruce Crampton,** professional golfer

43. Repair the green.

This is our sacred ground. Refer back to that karma thing. You do not want to mess with it here. Help to keep the green in top shape and never, ever take a divot from a green or carelessly toss a club or flagpole onto this sacred surface.

44. Respect the cart path rules.

Carts can be extremely damaging to the grass and can corrupt course playing conditions. The rules do apply to you. The "No Carts" signs are there for a reason; the groundskeepers know their stuff. No cart rules sign? Ask the pro shop or starter. Then use your common sense; you know if you are tearing up the course or not. Do not.

He who has the fastest golf cart never has a bad lie.

—**Mickey Mantle,** greatest baseball switch
hitter of all time and golfer

45. Play ready golf.

Be ready to play when it is your turn. Have your ball and club at the ready, keep your routine to a minimum, and take the shot. Always have an extra ball, tees, ball markers, and divot repair tools readily available. Never hold up other golfers with your game, a phone call, or anything else.

Most people play a fair game of golf. If you watch them.

—**Joey Adams,** comedian, author, and golfer

46. The ball is gone.

It is perfectly fine to look for a lost ball, but only for a few moments. Do not hold up the pace of play by looking for your ball for an extended time. Throw another ball down in the general area and resume play.

47. No one likes a braggart.

If you constantly point out your great shots or score, not many people will want to play with you again. It is good to praise other golfers; give them a chance to praise you.

We learn so many things from golf—how to suffer, for instance.
—**Bruce Lansky,** author and golfer

48. Admit you exaggerate the truth.

Do not get defensive and lie about lying. Golfers lie, or there are an incredible number of golfers who cannot count. Really, it is the truth. We are not lying.

Golf is a game in which the ball lies poorly and the players lie well.

—**Art Rosenbaum,** former *San Francisco Chronicle* sports editor and golfer

49. Ask nicely to play through.

If you want to play through, make sure there are not golfers in front of the ones you want to pass. Then, ask nicely. If the players in front of you say no, be gracious and say thank you. Leave it at that.

Mistakes are part of the game. It's how well you recover from them that's the mark of a great player.

—**Alice Cooper,** rock star and
4-handicap golfer

50. It is not a race.

It is a game. Enjoy the nuances of the game, the challenges, the other golfers, nature, and the squirrels. Chill, dude—just keep up normal pace of play for the course you are on. If it is a slow day and you do not have golfers behind you, take your time and enjoy the day. After all, you are on a golf course and not behind a desk!

51. Do not offer unsolicited advice.

The thing that works for you may not necessarily work for another golfer. If you are playing strictly by the rule book, it is actually a two-stroke penalty to offer unsolicited advice.

Never take advice on your golf swing that you did not pay for.

—Unknown

52. Rake the bunkers.

Always enter and leave the bunker the closest to your ball as you can, taking the rake with you. Then rake the bunker when you are finished, and leave the rake in the trap at the edge of the grass. Some courses ask that you leave it on the grass; when in doubt, ask the starter.

53. Quit calling do-overs.

It is always nice when you have the chance to hit a better ball, known as a mulligan. First consider, though, the golfers you are playing with and how crowded the course is at that particular time. Do not hold up play. Decide in advance the maximum number of mulligans to allow yourself in one round—and then stick to it.

A "gimme" can best be defined as an agreement between two golfers, neither of whom can putt very well.

—Unknown

Equipment

Hurry to your shot, but do not hurry your shot.

—Unknown

54. Clean your clubs and grips.

Take care of your clubs, and they will take care of you. Clean them after every shot; take advantage of that cleaning time to have another Zen moment planning your next great shot. After the game, make sure you put your clubs away clean.

55. Invest in quality climate gear.

You will be happy you did—we promise. It is hard to hit a golf ball correctly when you are shivering wet or sweltering from head to toe. The secret to playing in bad weather is to be prepared for bad weather.

Storms only roll in when you are having the game of your life.
—One of Murphy's many laws

56. Play in golf shoes.

Do not skimp in this area. You can wear tennis shoes, but golf shoes will give you more stability when hitting the ball. Happy feet mean happy golf.

57. Fit your clubs with a PGA professional.

It really does make a difference if you use clubs that fit your swing. The right set of clubs, fitted just for you, will make a huge difference in your game. We are talking yards and yards here. Most pro shops and golf stores offer this service either free or for a nominal charge. If you really want to get better at golf, this is a must.

Do not be too proud to take a lesson. I am not.

—**Jack Nicklaus,** professional golfer

58. Never lose a club again.

Most golf clubs are lost and forgotten somewhere on or near the green. The next time you carry a couple of clubs up there with you, leave the extras on the ground between the hole and your cart or lay the club(s) across the flagpole on the ground. It is hard to miss them when you have to step over them or pick them up to replace the flag.

Why do we work so hard to feel so bad?

—**Hollis Stacy,** professional golfer

59. Use the correct golf ball.

Yes, this does make a *big* difference. The choice of golf balls can be overwhelming. Do a little research and figure out which ones work best for you. Read the box or ask a golf pro what ball he or she recommends for you. You were fitted properly for your clubs; now make sure you are fitted properly for your golf balls.

It does look like a very good exercise. But what is the little white ball for?

—**Ulysses S. Grant,** eighteenth president of the United States, after watching a beginner swing several times without making contact with the ball

60. Regrip your clubs once a season.

We know, you are looking at your grips right now and saying, "Why? They look and feel perfectly fine to me." Well then, regrip just one, and you will notice the difference—in your hands and in your swing. Most golfers keep the same grips for a lifetime of golf; these are the same golfers who will wonder how you got so much better so quickly.

The more I practice, the luckier I get.

—**Gary Player,** professional golfer

61. Invest in a range finder.

Even the best research and yardage book cannot tell you exactly where you are on any given course. A range finder will let you know exactly what kind of yardage you are looking at for your next shot and will help you choose the correct club for that shot. This helps you play your best and maintain pace of play. When you know the exact distance to the hole, or wherever you want to hit your ball, you make a better decision on which club to use.

Hit the shot you know you can hit, not the one you think you should.

—**Dr. Bob Rotella,** sports psychologist, performance coach, and golfer

62. Use a stroke counter.

It can be as simple as a small, plastic counter that hangs on your bag, or even an app on your mobile phone. When you are first starting out and your score is higher, this will help you keep up with the number of strokes you have taken.

Par is anything you want. I have a hole that is a par 23. I nearly birdied the damn thing.

—**Willie Nelson,** musician, golfer, and owner of the Pedernales Golf Course

63. Pack a glove.

Some people just play better with a glove, and others do not. Either way, carry a glove with you just in case you find you need one. It is better to be prepared than to suffer a bad shot because you did not have a glove handy. It does not hurt to have a spare as well. An extra, dry glove will come in handy on a rainy day.

Everyone cheats when they first start playing golf. A lot of people don't ever stop.

—**Frank Beard,** rock band ZZ Top
drummer and golfer

64. Change your spikes regularly.

The spikes, or cleats, on golf shoes give you stability, but they do wear out. You should replace them at least once a year, if not more. Would you drive a Ferrari with bald tires? Maybe even try a pair of spike-less golf shoes. See what works best for you and your game.

Every shot counts. The three-foot putt is as important as the 300-yard drive.

—**Henry Cotton,** professional golfer

65. Buy a quality travel bag.

Baggage attendants at airlines and hotels do not care about your clubs. Not a bit. Remember, you are going to play golf, and they are not. Invest in a protective travel bag that offers good protection for your priceless companions.

The best wood in the golf bag of an amateur is the pencil.

—Unknown

66. Label your clubs and your bag.

Put your contact information on each club and on your bag, as well as in the bag. Flying? Take a picture of your bag with your phone right before it disappears into the airline baggage cave. This will help others know what they are looking for while you are crying.

Golf is a game in which you yell "fore," shoot six, and write down five.

—**Paul Harvey,** radio broadcaster and golfer

The trouble that most of us find with the modern matched set of clubs is that they do not really seem to know any more about the game than the old ones did.

—**Robert Browning,** former editor of *Golf Magazine* and golfer

67. Protect your clubs.

If you take care of your clubs with head covers and a bag cover, your clubs will take care of you. Note: Character head covers are fun, but no one wants to hire a new CEO or VP with a Betty Boop head cover. No offense to Betty Boop. Just use your good judgment when you decide to trot those things out for a game.

68. Wear a hat.

This will not only protect your head and face from the sun, but will also keep the glare out of your eyes. Anything you can do to minimize distractions will improve your game. If a better game means wearing a hat, wear the hat.

69. Start with a clean towel.

It is always easier to clean your clubs after a "dirty" shot with a clean towel than a dirty one from your last game. If it is a wet day, you can dry your grips after each shot. It will also make you look better and more put-together on the course. A note from coauthor Aram: do not use Mom's nice washroom towels. Take my word for it; this will not end well.

70. Carry first aid basics.

Band-Aids, antiseptic wipes, athletic tape, pain relievers—hopefully you will never need these items, but you sure will be glad you have them when you need them as far from the clubhouse as you can be. That is when you usually find yourself in need.

71. Bug spray is your friend.

You could be in the most bug-free area in the entire world, and bugs will find you on a golf course. Take our word for it; have that spray with you. Or carry clothing dryer sheets, and wipe yourself down with one of those to keep bugs away. Really, it works.

Have you ever noticed what golf spells backwards?

—Al Boliska, comedian and golfer

Body

The manly sport of golf, where you can dress like a pimp and no one will care.

—**Robin Williams,** comedian, actor, and author of one of the funniest golf comedy routines of all time

72. Dress for golf success.

Pick a style that suits you and makes you feel like a pro. When you are comfortable in your clothing and your style, you can concentrate on your game and not your pants. Know and be respectful of the course rules on golf attire; many require a collared shirt, and many have a strict policy against jeans.

73. Wear a nonrestrictive outfit.

You do not want a big, billowing shirt or jacket to get in the way of that incredible swing you have perfected. Nor do you want to be wearing something so tight you can barely move. Do not let your clothes get in the way of your great golf game.

74. Drink lots of water.

Remember, that is the stuff we are 70 percent made of. Keep hydrated on the course, and you will be able to concentrate more on your game. You can never drink too much water on a golf course. No, beer does not count.

75. Keep your head down.

You have heard it a million times, but it really does make the difference between a good shot and another extra stroke to your score. The next time you watch pros play, watch their head. Not their swing, just their head. It never moves until they have finished their shot.

Nobody ever looked up and saw a good shot.

—**Don Herold,** *Love That Golf*

76. Set a golf fitness routine.

A fitness routine is great for the body; your game and your significant other will thank you as well. Lift weights, stretch, walk—all of these simple steps will improve your game and your health. Did you know you can actually stretch and watch your favorite television show at the same time? What a concept!

I have a tip that can take five strokes off anyone's game. It's called an eraser.

—**Arnold Palmer,** professional golfer

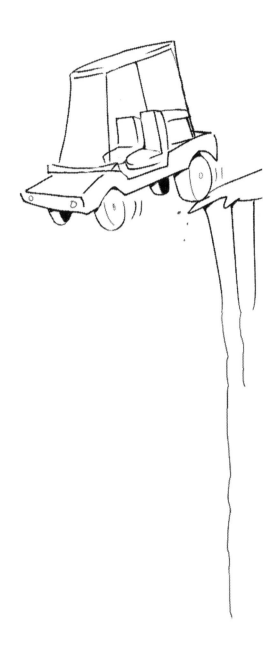

77. Ditch the golf cart.

Walking the course while you play is one of the most pleasurable things about golf. You can either get a walking cart for your clubs or carry them in a lighter-weight walking bag. It is great exercise, you can visualize your next shot as you are walking up to your ball, and you get to enjoy all that nature has to offer. Not only will this save you money, it will also improve your backside. Just remember to keep up pace of play!

78. Stretch your body.

Flexibility is key to your game and distance ... yes ... distance. Do yourself a big favor and stretch prior to your game. This is probably more important than any practice swings you take. Stretch after a round as well.

79. Eat healthy.

A heavy breakfast or lunch before a round of golf will weigh you down—literally. Soft drinks and sugary foods will also affect your game. When the snack cart comes around, half a turkey sandwich without the chips and a bag of plain peanuts will serve you better in the long run. When the game is over, then treat yourself to that hot dog!

80. Do not over-practice.

Extensive practice right before a round generally does not help your game and may serve to wear you out before you have even started. A pregame warm-up is just a warm-up to loosen your body and awaken your inner athlete. Take a few swings with a wedge, an iron, a hybrid, and your driver. Add a putting practice, and you are good to go.

81. Stay out of the sun.

Okay, that is not easy to do on a golf course, but four and a half hours of peak sun will burn anyone, anywhere on the planet. Even on a cloudy day, protect your skin and your eyes with sunscreen and sunglasses. The longer your skin and eyes last, the longer you last. That gives you so much more time for golf.

Don't play too much golf. Two rounds a day are plenty.

—**Harry Vardon,** professional golfer

Community

If ye can enjoy the walkin', ye can probably enjoy the other times in yer life when ye're in between. And that's most o' the time; wouldn't ye say?

—**Michael Murphy,** *Golf in the Kingdom*

82. Play different courses.

Who wants to be stuck in a rut? It is not only more entertaining to play different courses, it will also improve your confidence, which in turn will improve your game.

I had played so poorly recently, I started thinking that maybe I should do something else. Then I saw my friends going to work every day and realized that my life wasn't so bad.

—**Steve Pate,** professional golfer

83. Get your family and friends involved.

Being with friends and family is one of the greater joys of golf. The next thing you know, you are planning family vacations around golf courses. It is also how Rory, Tiger, and many other golf "names" began.

84. Play with strangers.

This will have the same effect on your game as playing different courses. You improve your confidence and learn a few new things; the end result is an improved game. Plus, you never know whom you could meet—a new partner, a best friend, or maybe a love interest.

If you think it is hard to meet new people, try picking up the wrong golf ball.

—**Jack Lemmon,** actor and golfer

85. Look up golf jokes.

Everyone loves a comedian, and it will keep you from taking this crazy game quite so seriously. No one wants to play golf with a crybaby. Memorize every line in the movie *Caddyshack*, and you will be good to go!

"Honey, do you think I can get to the green with a 6-iron?"
"Yes, dear. Eventually."

—**Cathy Arroyo to Sid Arroyo,** golfers and
husband and wife

86. Attend a professional golf event.

You can find a golf event just about anywhere on the planet. It is great fun to watch the pros do their thing. It is also good for your game to see that even the pros have the occasional bad shot. You may even learn a thing or two.

I tell myself that Jack Nicklaus probably has a lousy curveball.
—**Bob Walk,** MLB pitcher and golfer

87. Do not drink and drive.

When you drink alcohol on the course, you do not play as well, there is a lapse in safety precautions, you do not drive the cart well, and you become a danger to yourself and others when you drive home. It is just a bad idea all the way around.

If you drink, do not drive. Do not even putt.

—**Dean Martin,** singer, actor, and golfer

88. Don't throw a tantrum.

First of all, it is a game. Second, no one likes a sore loser. Third, you look like an idiot. Would you like us to go on with the list? We didn't think so. Also, it is hard to play golf when you have thrown your clubs in a lake.

89. Make small wagers or bets.

Adding a little competition among friends adds to the fun and helps you remember to not take things quite so seriously. It can be as simple as a couple of dollars or a beer after the game, just make sure you keep up with the pace of play.

You don't know what pressure is until you play for five bucks with only two bucks in your pocket.

—Lee Trevino, professional golfer

90. Volunteer your free time.

Help out at a charity or junior tournament. Take a group of kids who might otherwise never be exposed to the game to a course driving range. Remember, you are adding to the joy of thousands of people and giving back to the game. If karma holds true, the game will then give back to you, and we can all use a little good karma on the course.

Why am I using a new putter? Because the last one didn't float too well.

—**Craig Stadler,** professional golfer

91. Say yes to charity tournaments.

Fund-raising tournaments almost always make for a fun, easy golf game format that helps the game go easy on your ego and raises money for a good cause at the same time. Usually your level of ability is not so much a factor as what donation you are willing to give.

Enjoy the process, enjoy the opportunity to play.

—**Wendy Ward,** professional golfer

92. Get to know people at your favorite course.

If you play a course often, make a point of meeting others who play the course often, as well as the staff. You may learn something, and you just might find yourself with an incredible networking opportunity. By the way, the staff always welcomes cookies.

Can I play through?

93. Join a league or club.

Now that you have gotten to know others at your favorite course, consider becoming a member. It is comforting to have a home course, and you also support your local golfing community by joining the club. A win-win for everyone.

I do not care to join a club that is prepared to have me as a member.

—**Groucho Marx,** comedian, actor, and golfer

94. Remember *"Fore."*

This is the universal sign for golfers to turn away and cover their heads with their arms. Have you ever been hit in the head with a golf ball? No? Would you like to? I did not think so. Give other golfers the same common courtesy.

95. Practice golf with a friend.

It can be a lot more fun with a little friendly competition, you get a chance to catch up, and there is usually a nice walk involved.

Golf is very much like a love affair. If you do not take it seriously, it is no fun. If you do, it breaks your heart. Do not break your heart but flirt with the possibility.

—**Louise Suggs,** professional golfer and one of the founders of the Ladies Professional Golf Association (LPGA) Tour

96. Introduce someone to golf.

That is the great thing about golf—you can start to learn it and play it at any age. You may just start a passion for another, and you will have created another person to call when you are ready to play.

I prefer to take out the dog.

—**England's Princess Anne** on golf

97. Play with better players.

If you want to be a rock star, hang out with other rock stars. If you want to succeed in business, hang out with successful businesspeople. If you want to be a better golfer, play with better golfers. If you are the better player, be patient with the rest of us.

The best way to play better golf is to start younger.

—Unknown

98. Have fun.

We cannot say it enough. It is a *game*. Isn't the purpose of a game to have fun?

Don't force your kids into sports. I never was. To this day, my dad has never asked me to go play golf. I ask him. It's the child's desire to play that matters, not the parent's desire to have the child play. Fun. Keep it fun.

—**Tiger Woods,** professional golfer

99. Thank your partners.

Always thank your playing partners on the last green you play. Watch the bone-crushing "look how strong I am" handshake. It is not needed, it hurts, and you could actually damage the hand of another player.

Golf is a lot like life. When you make a decision, stick with it.
                                    —**Byron Nelson,** professional golfer

100. Get a good night's sleep.

If you are lucky, you have a golf game early in the morning. Getting a good night's rest, followed by a healthy, light breakfast, will put you in fine form for your next game.

If I am on the golf course and lightning strikes, I get inside fast. If God wants to play through, let him.

—**Bob Hope,** comedian, actor, and golfer

101. Judge yourself fairly.

When tracking your progress, judge yourself by where you were a year ago—not yesterday, not last week, not even last month. Look at how much you have improved in this last year and think positively about what you can do in the year ahead of you. Now, start back at tip #1 and have a great game!

One of the most fascinating things about golf is how it reflects the cycle of life. No matter what you shoot—the next day you have to go back to the first tee and begin all over again and make yourself into something.

—**Peter Jacobsen,** professional golfer

Got more dirt than ball. Here we go again.

—**Alan Shepard,** Apollo 14
commander and golfer, after
hitting the first ball on the
surface of the moon

The Wind Down

Ready, set, go! Okay, now I expect you to follow all these 101 tips by tomorrow and be a scratch player overnight. Got it?

Good!

Of course I am joking, but as an endnote to this book, this is a good point to bring up. We have established these 101 tips for golf success, but now what do we do with this information? Will completing every one of the 101 tips we covered automatically make you reach your goals? Maybe, but maybe not.

The important thing to remember is that fulfillment does not come in the end result, which of course is unique and different for everyone. The powerful message behind these quick and simple tips is the process. It is the idea that if we put energy and intent into improving, if we search for information and act on what we believe will make us better at what we do, we have already succeeded. And as a *result* of this investment, as a result of us internalizing that we want to improve, there is no possible way we will not improve.

I teach an average client base of about a hundred men and women, which accounts for close to two thousand lessons a year! And what I have taken and learned from my students is when we enjoy the process of improving and own it, making it our own, taking what we believe will make us successful, discarding what we believe does not apply to us, and applying our own unique ideas, we will have the best possible chance to reach our goals—*or* far exceed them. The sky is the limit!

As you sit and digest what you have just read, I would make this suggestion to you: oftentimes, the most powerful actions we can make are simple and effortless. There is a good chance you are already doing a lot of things this book outlines. Your first step is to analyze what out of these 101 golf tips you are already doing, and then start adding to the list as you see fit in order of priority. Trust your intuition and have fun with it!

Completing these tips should not feel like a chore; it should be exciting! Don't be too rigid. Make sure you personalize each of these suggestions to yourself, your golf habits, and your life schedule. Finally, make sure you track your progress and tweak your habits as needed. If you do this, there is an overwhelming chance you will see strokes melt away from your game. If not, at least you had a little more fun trying.

I will leave you with this: I work five days a week around eight to nine hours a day and oftentimes come in early and stay late. On my days off, I usually play with students. I answer phone calls and e-mails on my cell phone any time of day or night and have an app on my phone that keeps me connected to my company's internal website. I enjoy watching the Golf Channel, reading instructional books and magazines, and swinging my clubs in the house on my time off. Most would say I work a lot. I would counter and say I don't work at all, simply because my job is not work to me. I love what I do every day. I am chasing my dream! Every day I have the chance to add value to my students' lives. Every day I learn a vast amount of information on how to better coach, and every day I have fun. And I am not talking little sparks. I get fired up, energized, and motivated!

I am successful because I enjoy the process. I have my end goals and dreams I strive to achieve, but if I never get there, I still wake up a winner and successful because I love what I do on a daily basis.

—**Aram Hudson,**
PGA Professional,
rock star golf coach,
and co-author

Swinging at daisies is like playing electric guitar with a tennis racket; if it were that easy, we could all be Jerry Garcia. The ball changes everything.

—**Michael Bamberger,** author, sportswriter, and golfer

Checklist

1. Visualize the course before you play.
2. Arrive early.
3. Set tangible goals.
4. Be in the moment.
5. Create your own confidence.
6. Forget the last shot.
7. Do not count penalties.
8. Research the course.
9. Match the tee box to your ability.
10. Do not blame the club.
11. Ignore swing thoughts while you play.
12. Keep a golf journal.
13. Emphasize the good.
14. Separate practice from play.
15. Practice putting before a round.
16. Play a "one of two best balls" format.
17. Think strategically, like a chess player.
18. Create a preshot routine.
19. Practice trouble shots.
20. Learn from every round.
21. Increase your driver loft.
22. Buy a yardage book.
23. Learn your clubs.
24. Practice the shots you dislike.

25.   Video record your swing.

26.   Play *your* game.

27.   Practice short-game shots.

28.   Practice bunker shots.

29.   Take your medicine.

30.   Find the short grass.

31.   Know where to miss.

32.   Play smart golf.

33.   Putt when you can.

34.   Take lessons.

35.   Know the rules and etiquette of golf.

36.   Be quiet and considerate of others.

37.   Leave the course better than you found it.

38.   Be aware of the putting line.

39.   Keep up the pace.

40.   Let faster players play through.

41.   Watch your swing path and theirs.

42.   Praise other golfers.

43.   Repair the green.

44.   Respect the cart path rules.

45.   Play ready golf.

46.   The ball is gone.

47.   No one likes a braggart.

48.   Admit you exaggerate the truth.

49.   Ask nicely to play through.

50.   It is not a race.

51.   Do not offer unsolicited advice.

52.   Rake the bunkers.

53. Quit calling do-overs.

54. Clean your clubs and grips.

55. Invest in quality climate gear.

56. Play in golf shoes.

57. Fit your clubs with a PGA professional.

58. Never lose a club again.

59. Use the correct golf ball.

60. Regrip your clubs once a season.

61. Invest in a range finder.

62. Use a stroke counter.

63. Pack a glove.

64. Change your spikes regularly.

65. Buy a quality travel bag.

66. Label your clubs and your bag.

67. Protect your clubs.

68. Wear a hat.

69. Start with a clean towel.

70. Carry first aid basics.

71. Bug spray is your friend.

72. Dress for golf success.

73. Wear a nonrestrictive outfit.

74. Drink lots of water.

75. Keep your head down.

76. Set a golf fitness routine.

77. Ditch the golf cart.

78. Stretch your body.

79. Eat healthy.

80. Do not over-practice.

81.   Stay out of the sun.

82.   Play different courses.

83.   Get your family and friends involved.

84.   Play with strangers.

85.   Look up golf jokes.

86.   Attend a professional golf event.

87.   Do not drink and drive.

88.   Don't throw a tantrum.

89.   Make small wagers or bets.

90.   Volunteer your free time.

91.   Say yes to charity tournaments.

92.   Get to know people at your favorite course.

93.   Join a league or club.

94.   Remember "*Fore.*"

95.   Practice golf with a friend.

96.   Introduce someone to golf.

97.   Play with better players.

98.   Have fun.

99.   Thank your partners.

100. Get a good night's sleep.

101. Judge yourself fairly.

Download a free printable copy of this checklist at
www.yourdailysuccesstip.com/golf

I know I am getting better at golf because I am hitting fewer spectators.

—President Gerald Ford

The safest place would be in the fairway.

—Joe Garagiola, MLB player, TV
host, and golfer, on the best place
for spectators to stand during a
celebrity golf tournament

The Players

When she is not playing golf, **Dayna Steele** is a leading author-ity on business and success trends, including social media, networking, and customer service, as well as a rock radio Hall of Famer, CEO of YourDailySuccessTip.com, and au-thor of the 101 Ways to Rock Your  World book series. She writes for FastCompany.com, consults Fortune 500 companies, and is a popular key-note speaker. Her handicap is high. For more informa-tion, visit her page on www.yourdailysuccesstip.com.

 **Aram Hudson** discovered the game of golf at twelve. Coming from a non-golfing family, Aram discovered his passion for the game when his mother bought him a wooden club and some cheap balls from Goodwill to whack off of a mountain on a hike. From the first smack of the Arnold Palmer persimmon wood and cut-up Top Flight ball, he was hooked. At the University of New Mexico business department and the PGA/

PGM Golf Management Program, Aram was elected as a class A PGA professional. He is currently a certified golf instructor with GolfTec.

Cathy Arroyo started her golf journey when she bought an eight iron at a department store in 1985. An LPGA golf professional taught her how to keep her head down, her hands quiet, her hips rotating, and her eye on the ball. But it was raising her  daughter playing golf that taught Cathy how to play the game with passion, play by the rules, and understand the importance of sharing her love of the sport.

 **Tim Griggs** is an American pop artist and the cocreator of *Flashism,* a highly theoretical art movement that satirizes fear-mongering and paranoia in pop culture and subverts distinctions between high and low art, while reimagining the Internet and social networks as components of a larger creative fiction medium in which characters—both real and imagined—reject a world as it is in favor of one that is as they would make it. Visit www.timgriggsgallery.com for more confusion.

"Play it as it lies" is one of the fundamental dictates of golf. The other is *"Wear it if it clashes."*

—**Henry Beard,** humorist, author, and golfer

Want a free e-copy of the original *101 Ways to Rock Your World: Everyday Activities for Success Every Day***?** Sign up at YourDailySuccessTip.com ... for a lifetime of success!

Have an idea for a 101 Ways to Rock Your World book or would like to collaborate on a future edition? Contact dayna@yourdailysuccesstip.com.

Steele Media Services also offers a private edition of *101 Ways to Rock Your World* **as a companion piece to company employee handbooks.** Working closely with your HR and marketing departments, Dayna Steele creates a fun and insightful piece that includes your company history and mission. Contact dayna@yourdailysuccesstip.com for more information and pricing.

Contact:
Steele Media Services
1600 2nd Avenue
Suite 72
Seabrook TX 77586

A Final Thought

Years ago I had the opportunity to interview the legendary Walter Cronkite. We got on the subject of things he liked about Houston, one of those being Hermann Park. I mentioned there was a lot of controversy at the time over the number of trees they were planning to cut down. Cronkite commented on what a shame that was and asked why. I replied, "They are remodeling the golf course," to which one of the most recognizable voices in the world replied with a hearty laugh and said, "Oh, then that is fine. Take 'em all; cut 'em all down."

And that's the way it is.

—**Dayna Steele**